bite me

by

anne fitzgibbon

bee cooke

eleanor robinson

emily woolley

franky green

hariett lubin

katrina hinrichsen

lili hamlyn

lily stein

lydia pattihis

natasha eisner

phoebe hainsworth

rowan lennox

tamison o'connor

tammy perl

bite me books

ISBN no. 978-0-9564977-0-3

published by **bite me** books, 25 rathbone street, london w1t 1nq, england

copyright © 2010 **bite me** books

introduction

Food is a crucial part of human life – we need it, we depend on it. So why shouldn't we enjoy it? Our culture has become one of diet obsession and food paranoia; gone are the days when granny was the go-to woman when it came to cooking – now no one dares go near her recipes, for fear of discovering we've blacklisted half the ingredients! This really doesn't seem fair; we are setting the precedent for the future, teaching our children to be scared of food, rather than to see it for what it truly is: something to be enjoyed. On the other end of the spectrum is overindulgence. Every once in a while it doesn't hurt to treat yourself to that piece of chocolate cake, or have that second biscuit, but it's important to recognise the fine line that exists between satisfaction and gluttony. It's important to strike that balance: 'Everything in moderation', as they say.

Our aim is to encourage you to be active when it comes to the foods you eat – take an interest, take pleasure in what you're eating and make sure you're eating healthily. We've done all the hard work for you by selecting the yummiest recipes that are (mostly) healthy. Plus they're easy to prepare, so "I can't cook" is no excuse.

As teenagers ourselves, we understand the immense pressure young people can feel under to look perfect, but through the process of compiling this book, we have learned that happiness comes with good health, and good health comes with our cookbook.

the bite me team

contents

healthy bites	7
(not so) healthy bites	19
monster bites	31
brain bytes	41
global bites	49
party bites	67
liquid bites	79
starbites	85

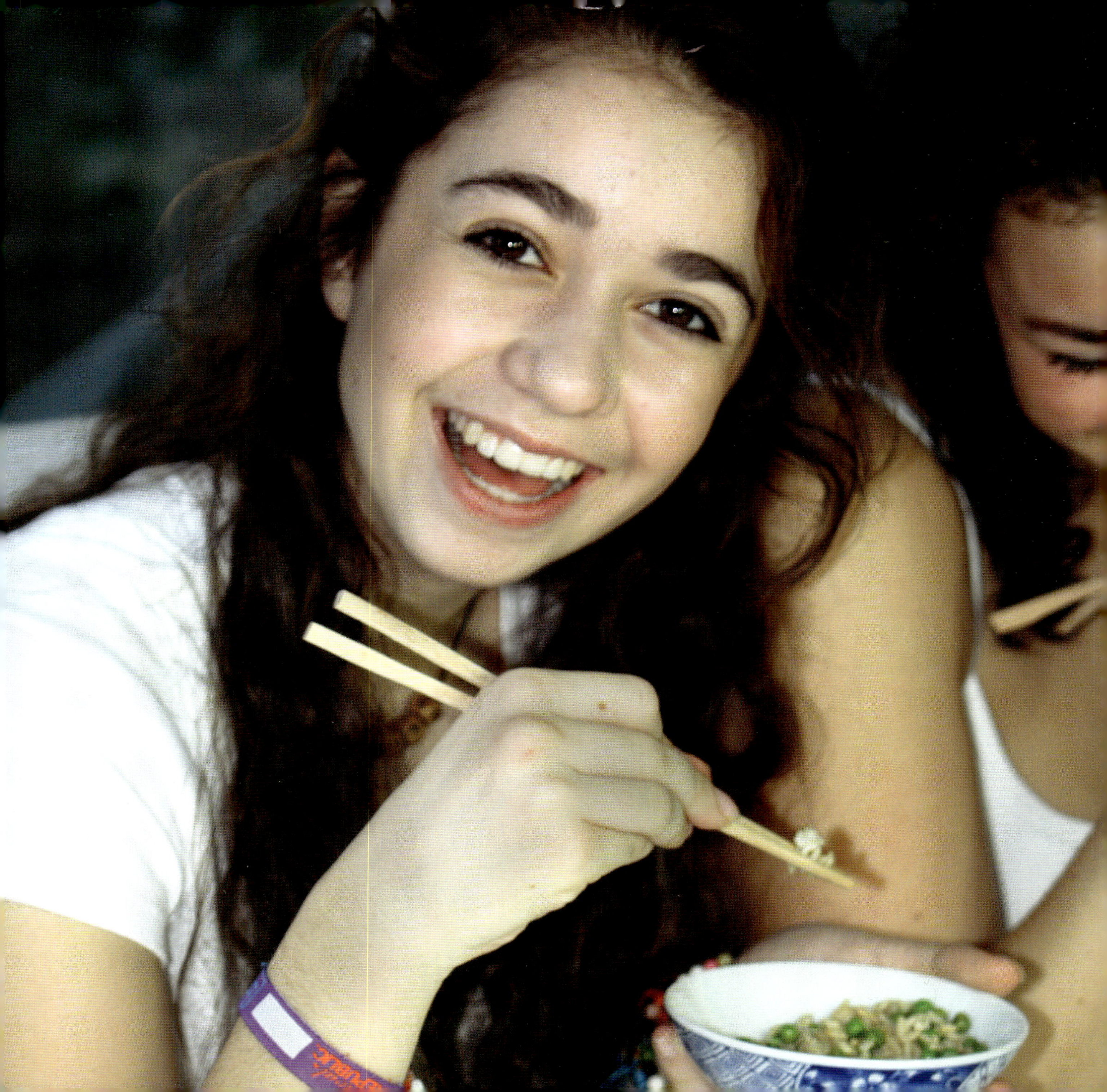

healthy bites

carrot & coriander soup

cold watercress & apple soup

summer soup

wintry pot of gold soup

cannellini & tuna salad

tuna & pasta salad

noodle salad with traditional dressing

greek salad wrap

spicy rice

bruschetta

egg fried rice

banana in overcoat

berry frozen yogurt slice

HEALTHY BITES

1

carrot and coriander soup

Peel and slice carrots. Peel and chop onion. Melt butter in pan and stir in carrots and onion. Cook gently for 2-3 minutes or until onion begins to soften.

Season with salt, pepper and add the sugar. Add coriander seeds - crushed with pestle and mortar or ground in peppermill (or ground coriander).

Pour in stock and bring to boil. Lower heat and cover. Simmer for 15 minutes or until the carrots are tender. Liquidise.

Add orange juice to the puree. Thin with the milk and continue heating until piping hot.

Sprinkle with chopped coriander, then serve with croutons.

500 g carrots
1 medium onion
50 g butter
1 tsp sugar
1 tbs crushed coriander seeds
1 l stock
juice of half an orange
125 ml whole milk

to finish:
chopped fresh coriander
croutons

cold watercress & apple soup

Melt the butter, add onion and cook until soft but not brown. Stir in watercress (keeping a few leaves for garnish) stock and curry powder.

Add cornflour mixed with a little water, bring to the boil and simmer for 8 minutes.

Add egg yolks to the hot cream and stir gradually into the soup with a whisk.

Remove from heat immediately and transfer to blender with one apple peeled, cored and sliced. Blend until smooth. Season to taste and chill thoroughly

For garnish, dice the remaining apple and soak in the lemon juice to keep the colour. Add to the soup before serving with a few watercress leaves for colour.

serves 4

2 tbs butter
1 tsp corn flour
1 tsp med. curry powder
1 bunch watercress
2 egg yolks
2 eating apples
2 Spanish onions, chopped
500 ml chicken or vegetable stock
125 ml hot double cream
juice of half a lemon
salt & white pepper

3 summer soup

900 g courgettes
1 medium onion
2 cloves garlic
3 ripe tomatoes
60 g butter
2 tbs olive oil
500 ml vegetable or chicken stock

Chop onion and garlic.
Sweat in melted butter and oil.
Add courgettes when softened.
Stir and cover and leave over very low heat.
Shake pan occasionally to mix flavours.
Skin and de-seed tomatoes, chop roughly and add.
to courgettes when they have softened.
Cook briefly together.
Liquidise.
Bring to required consistency with stock.
Re-heat and serve.

wintery pot of gold soup

Preheat oven to 240° C

Brush the squash wedges with olive oil and put them on a roasting tray. Dot the squash with garlic purée and roast for 45 minutes. Allow to cool and peel off all the skin.

Heat the olive oil in a large saucepan. Add the onions and carrots and cook gently for 10-15 minutes or until the vegetables are soft but not brown.

Pour the stock onto the vegetables and bring to the boil. Turn down the heat and let simmer for 20 minutes or until tender.

Add the squash, vegetables and cream and simmer for 5 more minutes

Blend until smooth, stir in honey, heat gently and serve.

5

cannellini & tuna salad

250 g tin cannellini beans
2 x 200 g tins tuna in oil
25 g rocket
4 baby spring onions, peeled & sliced thinly
sea salt & black pepper

for the dressing:
grated zest & juice of 1 lemon
2 cloves garlic, peeled & crushed
1 tsp of mustard
3 tbsp olive oil
3 tbsp tuna oil, reserved from the tins of tuna
sea salt & black pepper

french bread. warmed

Drain the tuna over a bowl, retaining the oil.

To make the dressing, mix the crushed garlic with the mustard and a little salt and black pepper. Add the grated lemon zest and then the lemon juice, olive oil and tuna oil. Mix everything together thoroughly with a fork and pour over the beans. Stir well.

To serve, arrange roughly three-quarters of the rocket leaves over the base of a dish. Spoon the beans on top and scatter the tuna fish on top in small chunks. Use the remaining rocket leaves to add colour to the top of the dish. Sprinkle the spring onion slices on top. Add more lemon zest, if desired, to garnish.

Serve with warm, crusty French bread.

tuna & pasta salad

Fill a saucepan with water and add a pinch of salt and one tablespoon of oil. Cover and bring to the boil. Tip in the pasta bows into the boiling water and stir. Leave on medium heat for 10 minutes.

To make the dressing, mix together the oil, mustard, vinegar and season with salt and pepper.

Drain the pasta in a colander, and leave to cool. Rinse the beans and drain. Mix together in a bowl and add the dressing.

Cut the roots and the green part off the spring onions and chop. Snip the tops off the cress and cut the chives into small pieces and add to spring onions. Drain the tuna.

Add the cress, spring onions, chives, beans and tuna to the cooled pasta.

To serve: if you like, add salad leaves

salt
1 tbsp sunflower oil
100 g pasta bows
125 ml sunflower oil
3 tbsp wine vinegar
1 tsp French mustard
freshly ground black pepper
432 g tin flageolet beans
3 spring onions
1 punnet of cress
1 small packet of fresh chives
200 g tinned tuna
15 pitted black olives
salad leaves *(optional)*

7

noodle salad with traditional dressing

serves 6

200 g asparagus tips, halved vertically

3 spring onions

3 cm ginger, peeled & grated

2 tsp vegetable oil

1 tsp sesame oil

1 small red chilli, deseeded & chopped

4 tbsp soy sauce

200 g mange tout/sugar snaps

250 g of thin rice noodles

Boil a pan of water and blanch (cook lightly) the asparagus and mange tout/sugar snaps for 2 minutes. Drain and put in cool water.

Put the noodles in a bowl full of boiling water and set aside for 7 minutes to soak. Drain and place in cool water and then return to the bowl.

Add the soy sauce, chilli, spring onions, asparagus, mange tout/sugar snaps and oils to the noodles. Toss and serve.

8

greek salad wrap

75 g chopped feta cheese

1 red peppers, chopped

1/4 cucumber, chopped

a few kalamata olives

a drizzle of olive oil

1 tortilla wrap

tzaziki (*to taste*)

Place the pieces of cheese, peppers, cucumber, and olives on one end of the tortilla wrap.
Drizzle with olive oil.
Close up the other end of the wrap by rolling up tightly.
Delicious with tzatski *(see page 59)*.

spicy rice

9

Heat oven to 180° C.
Rinse and soak rice for 10 minutes.
Heat a large ovenproof saucepan on gas or electric hob.
Add the oil, then the onions, garlic and ginger.
Cook on a low heat until the onion is soft.
Add the cloves, cinamon and caramom pods and cook for a further 2 minutes on a low heat.
Add the curry powder and cook for a further 2 minutes.
Stir mixture.
Drain the rice and add it to the saucepan.
Stir so that the rice is coated in the oil and spices.
Add the peas, sweetcorn and half the flaked almonds.
Pour in the stock and stir.
Cover the pan with a lid of sheet of foil and cook in the oven for 15-20 minutes.
Remove from oven and scatter the remaining almonds.

200 g basmati rice
1 tbsp sunflower oil
1 large onion, peeled & chopped
2 garlic cloves, peeled & sliced
1 thumb sized piece of ginger, peeled & chopped
2 whole cloves
1 cinnamon stick
2 cardamom pods, cracked
2 tsp medium curry powder
50 g frozen peas
50 g frozen sweetcorn
50 g flaked almonds
375 ml stock (1 stock cube dissolved in 375 ml boiling water)

HEALTHY BITES

10 bruschetta

6 ripe plum tomatoes
2 cloves garlic, minced
1 tbsp extra virgin olive oil
7 fresh basil leaves, chopped
1 baguette
1 tsp basalmic vinegar
60 ml olive oil

Preheat oven to 230° C. Chop tomatoes finely and mix with garlic, basil, 1 tbsp olive oil and basalmic vinegar. Salt and pepper to taste. Slice the baguette diagonally in 2 cm slices. Brush with olive oil, place on a baking sheet and toast for 5-6 minutes.

Spoon mixture on each slice of toast and serve.

11 egg fried rice

250 g uncooked instant rice
500 ml water
1 tbsp of sesame oil
soy sauce to taste
2 medium eggs, beaten
1 tbsp finely chopped ginger root
4 tbsp finely chopped spring onions
250 g fresh or frozen peas

Bring water to the boil in a medium saucepan.
Stir in the rice and cover.
When soft remove from the heat and leave to stand for 5 minutes.
Drain any excess water.
Heat oil in a large frying pan.
Stir in the rice and soy sauce.
Heat briefly then transfer the rice to a bowl.
Scramble the eggs in the same frying pan then stir in the rice.
Stir in the ginger, spring onions and peas, heat through and serve.

HEALTHY BITES

banana in overcoat

12

Peel a nice, ripe banana, and dip in Greek yoghurt. Roll in your favourite crushed cereal and freeze. Eat when frozen.

ripe banana
greek yoghurt
cereal

berry frozen yoghurt slice

13

Line a standard 900 g loaf tin with freezer film. Sift the icing sugar over the frozen raspberries or blueberries in a bowl and then drizzle over the honey. Stir well together and mix in the yoghurt and almonds.

Spoon into the lined loaf tin, levelling off the surface. Cover the top with freezer film and freeze overnight.

Turn out of the tin and, using a serrated or electric knife, cut into slices.

50 g icing sugar
280 g frozen raspberries/blueberries
4 tbsp clear honey
500 g plain low-fat yoghurt
70 g almonds

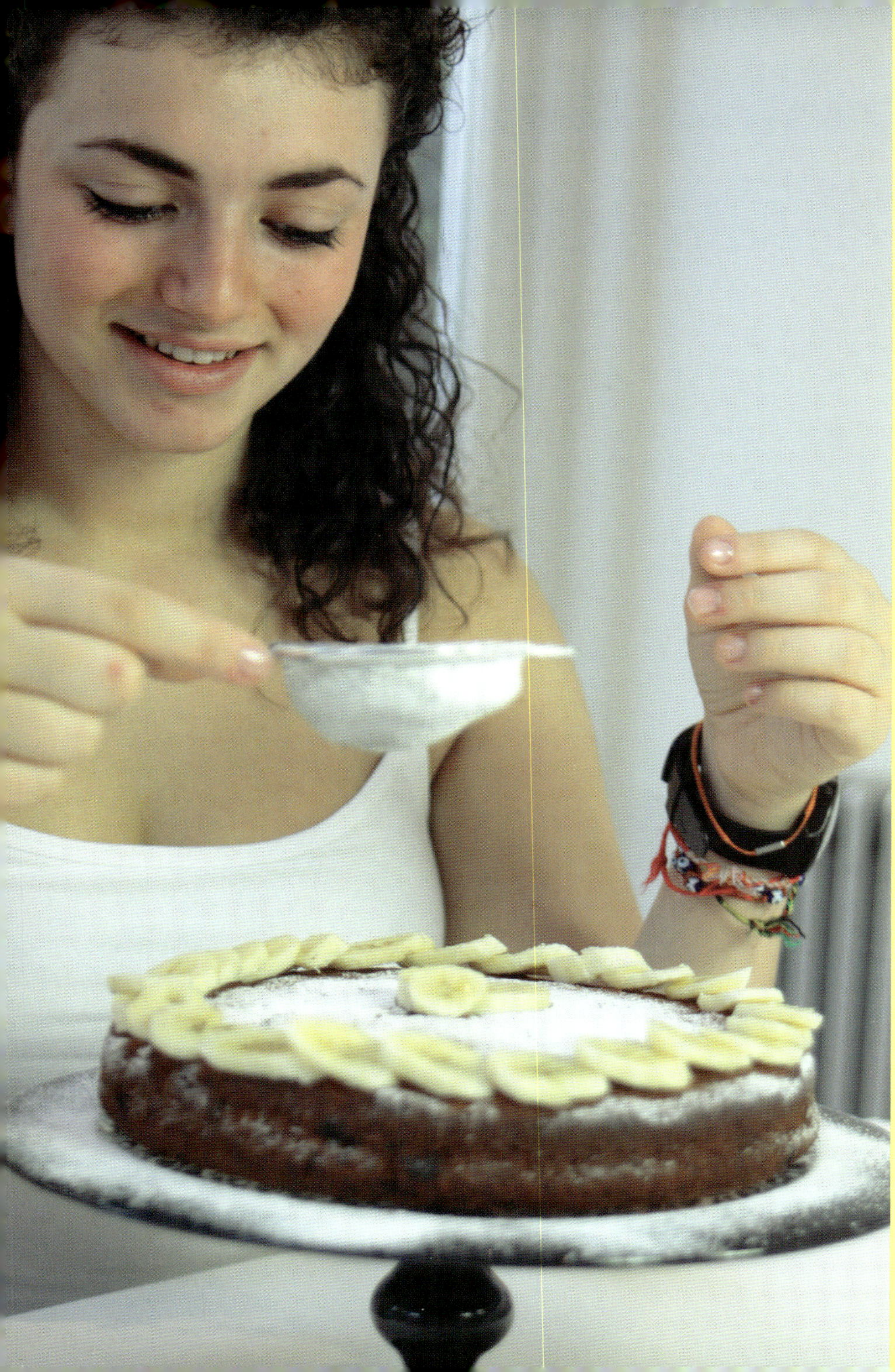

(not so) healthy bites

mediterranean scones

gingerbread biscuits

honey cake

chocolate fridge cake

chocolate peanut butter cheesecake bars

raisin & oatmeal cookies

rickety rocky road

best brownies

dear abby's pecan pie

ginger bites

1

mediterranean scones

350 g self-raising flour
1 tbsp baking powder
1/2 tsp salt
50 g butter
1 tbsp olive oil
8 halves sundried tomatoes (chopped)
100 g feta cheese
10 black olives, pitted and halved
300 ml full fat milk
1 egg, beaten

Heat oven to 200° C.
Grease a large baking sheet.
In a large bowl mix together the flour, baking powder and salt.
Rub in the butter with the oil until the mixture looks crumbly.
Now add the tomatoes, cheese and olives.
Make a well in the centre using a spoon and pour in the milk.
Mix with a knife using a cutting movement until it becomes a soft sticky dough.
Flour your hands and the work surface and shape the dough into a round shape about 4 cm thick.
Cut into eight wedges and place them apart on the baking sheet.
Brush with the beaten egg.
Bake for 15-20 minutes until risen, golden and springy to the touch.
Then remove spread with butter and eat.

gingerbread biscuits

2

Preheat the oven to 180° C.

Put the flour, ground ginger, butter and bicarbonate of soda in a mixing bowl. Mix with fingers until crumbly, then add the sugar, golden syrup and the egg. Mix until it forms a firm pastry mix.

Lightly flour your work surface and dust the rolling pin with flour. Roll the pastry out evenly, about 5mm thick.

Cut out your biscuits with festive Christmas cutters

Place them on a greased/non-stick baking tray, and place in oven when heated. Check after 10 minutes, but 15 minutes should cook them perfectly

You can serve plain or decorate with icing, raisins, chocolate chips, silver balls etc.

350 g plain flour
175 g soft brown sugar
95 g butter
1 medium sized egg
3 tbsp golden syrup
1 tsp bicarbonate of soda
3 tsp ground ginger
(optional) icing, raisins, silver balls and/or chocolate chips

and
rolling pin
Christmassy-shaped pastry cutters

3

honey cake

400 g self-raising flour
200 g caster sugar
250 ml golden syrup
250 ml corn oil
250 ml boiling water
1 tsp baking powder
1 tsp ground ginger
1 tsp mixed spice
1 tsp cinnamon
5 tsp orange juice
3 eggs

This is a typically Jewish dish served best at Jewish New Year (Rosh Hashannah) with apple and honey.

Preheat oven to 180° C. Grease and line two 900g loaf tins with greaseproof paper.

Combine the syrup, sugar and oil over heat until everything has melted. Remove from heat, add boiling water and stir. Cool slightly.

Place all the other ingredients in a mixing bowl and add the syrup mixture. Beat until everything is mixed together and is a light golden brown colour. Pour the mixture evenly into the two tins and bake for around an hour until a skewer inserted into the middle of the cake comes out clean.

For a delicious change, add two or three mashed bananas to the mixture or sprinkle a handful of chopped almonds onto the cake before it goes into the oven.

chocolate fridge cake

Use cling film to line a 20cm shallow, square-shaped tin.

Leave extra cling film hanging over the sides.

Bash the biscuits into pieces using a rolling pin. (Put them in a plastic bag first so they don't go everywhere!)

Melt chocolate, butter and golden syrup in a heatproof bowl set over a pan of simmering water. Stir occasionally. Remove the bowl from the heat and stir in the broken biscuits, apricots, raisins and pecans (optional).

Spoon the mixture into the tin. Level the surface by pressing it down with a potato masher.

Leave to cool, then put the chocolate mixture in the fridge for 1-2 hours to set.

Turn out the cake and peel off the cling film. Cut the cake into 12 squares and enjoy!

250 g digestive biscuits
150 g milk chocolate
150 g dark chocolate
100 g unsalted butter
150 g golden syrup
100 g dried chopped apricots
70 g raisins
60 g chopped pecans *(optional)*

preparation time less than 30 minutes
cooking time less than 10 minutes

5

chocolate peanut butter cheesecake bars

Base: Beat the cake mix, egg and melted butter until thick and doughy. Grease and dust with flour a 30 x 20 cms baking tray then spread the mixture evenly on the bottom.

Filling: Beat the cream cheese and peanut butter until smooth. Add the eggs, beat well, then add the icing sugar and butter. Continue to beat until the mixture is completely smooth. Spread the mixture evenly on the base. Bake for 30-35 minutes at 180° C.

Cool before cutting into bars.

for the base of the bars:
500 g box of chocolate cake mix
1 egg
110 g butter, melted

for the filling:
225 g cream cheese, room temperature
200 g smooth peanut butter
2 eggs
500 g powdered sugar
110 g butter, melted

raisin & oatmeal cookies

6

Turn the oven on and heat to 180° C.

Add the butter and sugar to a bowl and beat the mixture until it is pale and fluffy, then gradually add in the beaten egg. Sift in the flour and then fold it in with the oatmeal, chocolate chips and raisins.

Put large teaspoons of the mixture onto 3 greased baking sheets. (Make sure you leave enough space around each cookie, as they will spread out during baking.)

Bake for 10–15 minutes in the oven and take the cookies out when they are golden brown.

Allow them to cool slightly on the baking sheets and then transfer to a wire rack and leave to cool completely.

85 g unsalted butter
120 g sugar
1 egg (beaten)
115 g self raising flour
55 g medium oatmeal
100 g raisins
170 g chocolate chips

3 greased baking sheets
wire racks

makes roughly 18 cookies

7

rickety rockety road

400 g dark chocolate
150 g marshmallows
1 packet digestive biscuits
50 g dried cranberries

Grease and line a small baking tin.

Melt the chocolate in a bowl over a pan of lightly simmering water. When melted, set aside to cool slightly.

Place the biscuits in a strong plastic bag and bash with a rolling pin until you have fine crumbs.

Cut the marshmallows into small pieces and add with the crushed biscuits to the melted chocolate and stir, ensuring all is covered well with chocolate. Mix in the dried cranberries.

Place the mixture into the tin, pressing it down with the back of a spoon. Put into the fridge to set. When set, turn out and cut into small squares.

If you don't have marshmallows, use large-ish chunks of white chocolate - it is delicious.

best brownies

Preheat oven to 180° C. Grease and flour a 20 x 30 cm baking pan.

Melt butter and chocolate togethere in a saucepan over a low fire. When melted set aside to cool at room temperature.

Meanwhile, beat eggs and sugar until thick and lemon-coloured; add vanilla. Fold chocolate mixture into eggs and sugar. Mix thoroughly.

Sift flour and fold gently into batter, mixing just until blended.

Pour into the prepared pan. Bake for 25 minutes, or until centre is just set. Try not to overbake.

Allow brownies to cool in pan for 30 minutes before cutting into bars.

Makes 28 large brownies.

250 g butter
115 g green & black's cocoa
4 eggs
450 g caster sugar
115 g plain flour
1 tsp vanilla extract

9

dear abby's pecan pie

240 ml white corn syrup (use karo brand - from selfridges, harrods, partridges & other delis. Don't substitute with golden syrup.)

240 g dark brown sugar

1/3 tsp salt

75 g melted butter

1 tsp vanilla extract

3 whole eggs

150 g whole pecan halves (or walnuts)

Mix syrup, sugar, salt, butter, vanilla. Add slightly beaten eggs. Pour into a 9-inch unbaked pie shell. Sprinkle pecans over fillling. Bake in 180º C oven for approximately 45 minutes.

You can top it with a bit of whipped cream or ice cream, but even plain, nothing tops this!

This recipe is by Abigail Van Buren, America's most famous agony aunt.

ginger bites

Preheat the oven to 150° C, fan 140° C. Sift the flour into a bowl, then mix in the sugar, oats, ginger and bicarbonate of soda.

Heat the milk with the syrup and butter gently in a pan until the butter is melted then add to the bowl. Whisk these liquid ingredients into the dry ones already in the bowl.

Pour into prepared tin. Bake in the oven for about 45 minutes. Leave to cool and then cut into squares.

175 g plain flour
200 g caster sugar
110 g butter
3 tbsp golden syrup
2 tsp ground ginger
1 tsp bicarbonate of soda
125 g porridge oats
a lightly buttered tin lined with baking paper

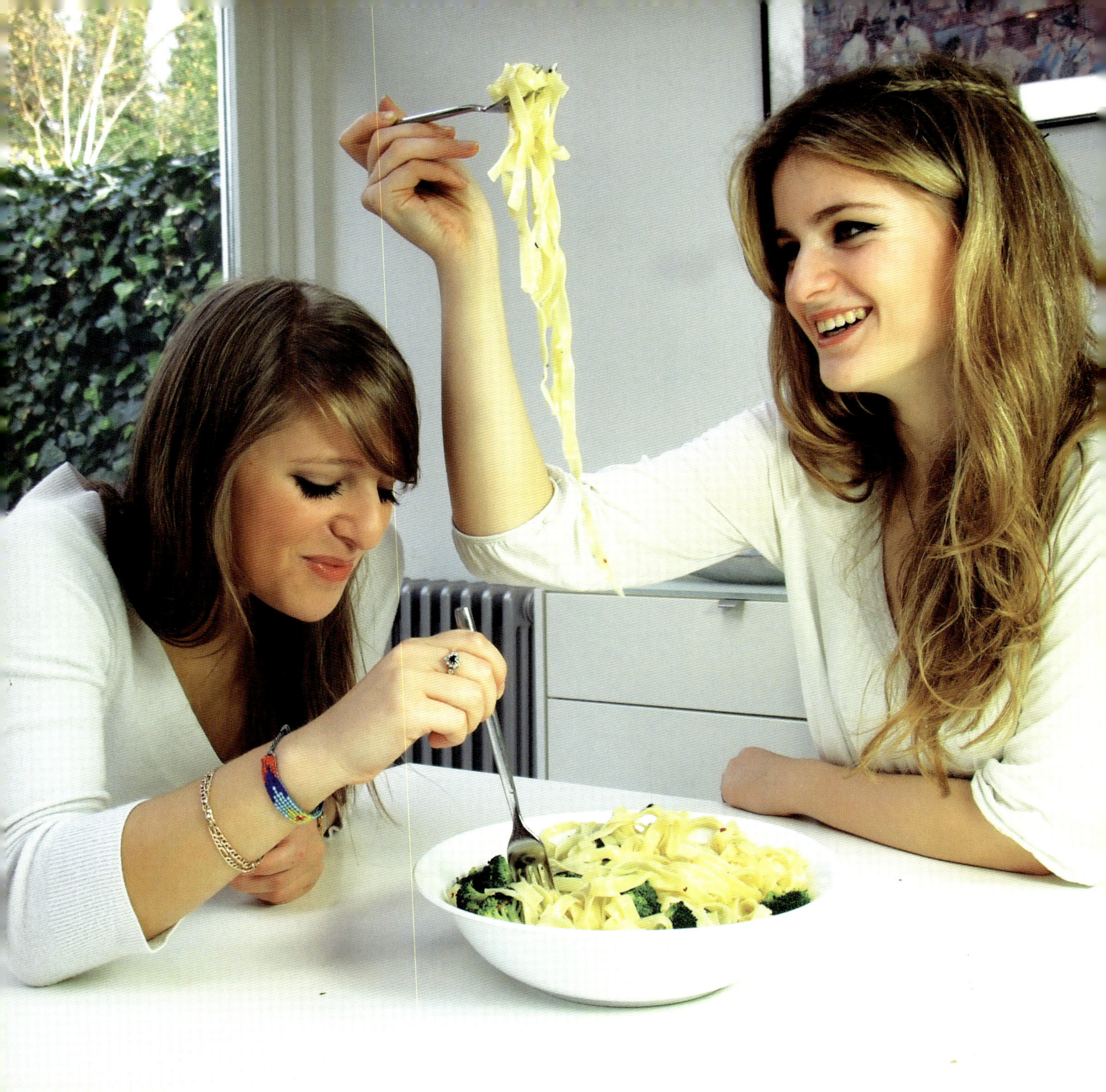

monster bites

grilled chicken strips

cottage pie

the ultimate steak sandwich

stuffed aubergine

barbecued chicken drumsticks

cheese omelette

sweet potato fritatta

broccoli chili pasta

1 grilled chicken strips

serves 6

prep time: 15 mins plus marinade for as long as possible

cook for 10 mins

1 kg chicken breasts, boned & skinned

for the marinade:

5 tbsp olive oil

4 tbsp red wine vinegar

1 medium onion, peeled & chopped

1 whole head of garlic, each clove peeled & chopped

2 cm cube fresh ginger, peeled & chopped

2 tbsp fennel seeds

2 tbsp ground cumin

2 tbsp ground corriander

seeds from 8 cardamom pods

1 tbsp ground cinnamon

8 whole cloves

20 black pepper corns

1/2 tbsp cayenne pepper (for a mildly hot dish)

salt to taste

1 tbsp tomato purée

Mix all the marinade ingredients together in a blender. Place the chicken strips in a bowl and pour over the marinade, stirring to ensure the chicken is fully coated. Cover with cling film.

Leave the chicken to marinade in the fridge for at least 3 hours, but preferably overnight.

Preheat the grill to high. Line a baking tray with aluminium foil and place the chicken strips on the foil. Grill for 10 minutes, then turn over and grill for another 10 minutes, until the chicken is lightly browned and thoroughly cooked.

cottage pie

2

Preheat oven to 200° C.

Filling: Place a large saucepan over medium heat, add beef mince and brown for 3 minutes. Add onion and carrot, then continue to cook until the meat is no longer pink and the onion begins to brown (about 5 more minutes). Add the flour and parsley.

In a small bowl, combine beef stock and tomato purée, then add to beef mixture. Add salt and pepper to taste. Lower heat and simmer mixture for 15 minutes, stirring occasionally, until almost all of the liquid has evaporated. Spoon mixture into a ceramic oven proof dish.

Potato topping: Put potatoes in a medium saucepan, cover with water and place over a high heat. Boil for 15 minutes (or until potatoes are tender). Drain.

Mash potatoes and add butter and milk and continue to mash until the mixture is smooth. Add salt and pepper to taste. Spread potatoes over beef filling and sprinkle with grated cheddar cheese.

Bake in pre-heated oven for 25 minutes until top is brown.

500g of lean beef mince
1 large onion, diced
3 carrots, diced
2 tbsp flour
2 tbsp chopped fresh parsley
350 ml beef stock
1 tbsp tomato purée
4 large potatoes, peeled & quartered
50 g butter
230 ml whole milk
125 g grated cheddar cheese
salt & pepper to taste

3

the ultimate steak sandwich

300 ml vegetable oil, for deep frying
large potato
sea salt

100 g rump steak, sliced
1 tsp olive oil, plus extra for drizzling
1 tbsp chopped fresh chives
baguette, sliced in half lengthways
tomato ketchup, to serve

For the chips, pour the vegetable oil into a saucepan or deep fat fryer and heat for 30 seconds.

Slice the potato into matchsticks and pat dry with kitchen paper. Carefully place the potato sticks into the hot oil and deep fry until crisp and golden. Remove with a slotted spoon, drain on kitchen paper and sprinkle with sea salt.

For the steak sandwich, rub the sliced steak with olive oil, salt and freshly ground black pepper and griddle in a very hot griddle pan for about a minute. Remove from the pan.

Drizzle the halved baguette with olive oil and griddle for about one minute on each side.

Serve with lashings of tomato ketchup and the fries and vegetables of your choice.

stuffed aubergine

4

Salt the aubergines before you start. Not only does this release bitter juices, but when salted, aubergines soak up less oil. Scoop out the aubergine and brush the inside of the skins with a little olive oil. Then cook in the oven for about 10 minutes.

Cube the scooped out aubergine, and then thinly cut up the onion and crush the garlic clove. Lightly fry the onion and garlic until softened. Then add the aubergine and carry on frying.

Cut a good amount of cherry tomatoes in half, adding them to the pan. Add some mushroom ketchup and cook until the aubergine and tomatoes have softened.

Put the mix into the aubergine skins, and top with sliced mozzarella. Grill for a few minutes. Finally, chop some fresh basil, sprinkle on top, and serve.

1 large aubergine
olive oil
1 small onion
1 garlic clove
18 cherry tomatoes
1 tbsp mushroom ketchup
125 g mozzarella
fresh basil

5

4 chicken drumsticks
2 tbsp of tomato ketchup
2 tbsp light soy sauce
2 tbsp clear honey
1 tbsp sunflower oil
2 tbsp lemon juice

salad leaves

barbequed chicken drumsticks

Make one or two slashes on the top of each drumstick. Mix together the ketchup, soy sauce, honey, oil and lemon juice into a large bowl. Add the drumsticks.

Make sure the chicken is covered in the sauce, and put in the fridge for a minimum of one hour, turning occasionally. Preheat the grill to high and put the chicken under the grill. Turn the grill down to medium and remove after 5 minutes. Brush extra sauce on the chicken and return to grill.

Repeat these steps until juices run clear when drumsticks are skewered.

Once cooked, serve on a plate with salad leaves.

cheese omelette

6

Put the eggs, herbs and salt and pepper into a bowl and mix with a fork, being careful not to whisk the mixture for more than about 30 seconds.

Heat the oil in the frying pan and then pour in the egg mixture and after 30 seconds or so mix the firming egg mixture in the pan. After another 30 seconds, sprinkle the cheese evenly over one half of the omelette.

Cook the omelette until the top has started to firm up and cheese is beginning to melt. This should take around a minute.

Flip the omelette over in half (the half without cheese to go over the half with cheese). Cook each side for a further 15 to 30 seconds or until each side is very light golden brown, before serving.

3 eggs
60 g cheese
1 tbsp olive oil
1 tsp of mixed herbs

7

sweet potato fritatta

serves 2

1 large sweet potato (approx. 250 g)
1 tbsp olive oil
1 shallot, peeled & finely chopped
4 large eggs
small handful chives, finely chopped
salt & pepper to taste

Peel the sweet potato and cut into 1cm cubes.

Put the oil into a frying pan over medium heat. When hot, add the sweet potato and shallot. Sprinkle with salt and pepper. Cook for about 5 minutes or until the edges turn slightly golden brown.

Beat the eggs in a bowl and add the chives. Pour the egg and chive mixture over the sweet potato mixture on the stove.

Cook for a few minutes without stirring the mixture. Once it has cooked, leave to cool for about a minute.

Then take a plastic spatula to remove the fritatta from the pan and place on a large plate. Cut into slices and serve.

broccoli chili pasta

Cut the broccoli into small florets, making sure to finely slice any thick stems and steam until broccoli is just tender. Boil the tagliatelle in lightly salted water according to packet instructions.

Whilst the pasta is cooking, finely chop the garlic and chili and combine with the olive oil in a small saucepan, briefly heating the mixture over a low heat. Then add the broccoli to the saucepan, taking it off the heat and mixing it making sure the broccoli is fully coated in the oil mixture. As well as giving a nice flavour to the dish, this mixture will prevent the pasta from sticking together.

Drain the pasta and add the broccoli and serve.

400 g tagliatelle
400 g broccoli
1 clove garlic, finely chopped
1 red chili, seeds removed
75 ml olive oil

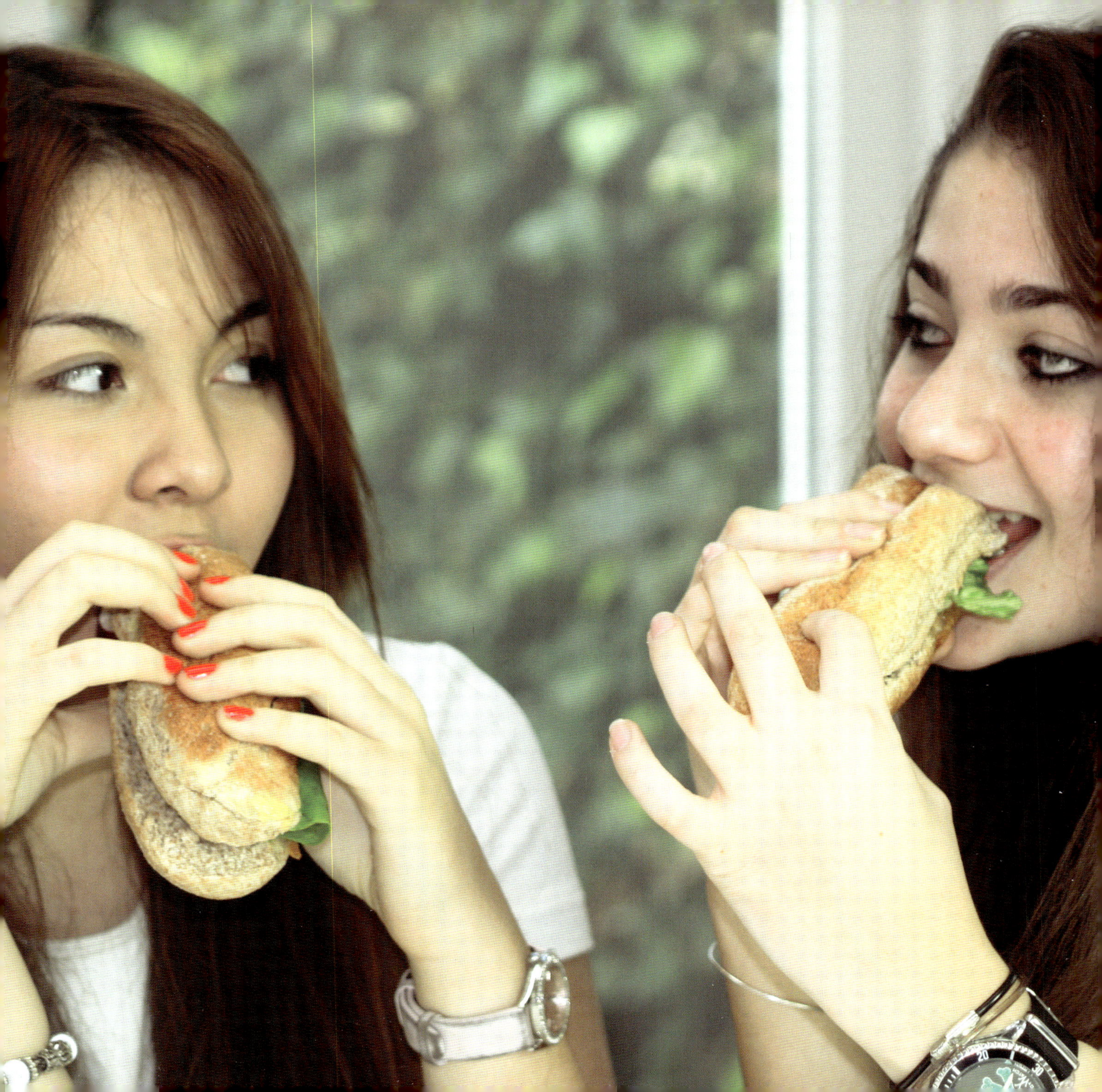

brain bytes

kippers & rice & peas

spicy prawn salad

smoked haddock pasta

salmon burgers

apple & honey muffins

blueberry crème brûlée

1

kippers & rice & peas

1 x 200 g packet of boil in bag smoked kipper fillets

150 g rice (basmati is best)

100 g frozen peas (petit pois is best)

piece of lemon

Fill a medium saucepan with water, place over medium heat and bring to the boil. Place the kipper fillets (in the bag) in the boiling water for about 5 minutes (or as long as packet specifies).

Meanwhile, place the rice and 350 ml of water in a small saucepan and bring to the boil. Turn down the heat and allow the rice to simmer with the lid on until all the water has evaporated.

Add the frozen peas to a saucepan of water and place over a medium heat. The peas are ready when they are soft but still bright green, be careful not to overcook or they become squishy.

Remove kippers from bag and serve with rice, peas and lemon to garnish.

spicy prawn salad

2

Cut the avocados in half, removing the skin and stone. Slice into four lengthways and place on plate.

Toss the cooked, cold prawns in the lemon juice, cumin, salt, black pepper, and olive oil and place on top of the avocados.

Mix all the ingredients for the dressing in a bowl and drizzle over salad.

6 large cooked king prawns
2 avocadoes
juice of 1 lemon
1/4 tsp cumin
1/4 tsp salt
1 /4 tsp freshly ground black pepper
1 1/2 tsp extra virgin olive oil

For the dressing
150 ml mayonnaise
50 ml ketchup
1 dash tabasco sauce
1 lemon, juice only
1 clove garlic, crushed

3 smoked haddock pasta

to poach the haddock:
500 g smoked haddock
240 ml milk
1 bay leaf
6 whole peppercorns
1/2 carrot
1/2 yellow onion
3 whole cloves

for the pasta:
cooked rigatoni pasta
500 g crème fraiche
fresh zest of 1-2 lemons
salt & pepper
3 spring onions, chopped
handful of fresh flat-leaf parsley, chopped
2 steamed carrots, cut in coins
250 g steamed petit pois

Put the milk, bay leaf, peppercorns, carrot, onion (with cloves studded into it) and the smoked haddock (skin facing upwards) in a saucepan. Bring to a gentle simmer for 5 minutes and turn off the heat to cool. Then take the fish off the skin in large chunks and set aside in a bowl. Reserve the milk liquid in case you need some to moisten the pasta later.

Cook pasta according to directions on the packet.

In a large serving bowl, mix together the crème fraiche, lemon zest, pepper, spring onions and parsley. Add the pasta, carrot coins, petit pois and fish chunks and mix together gently. If it seems a little dry, add the strained poaching liquid.

This dish is delicious warm or cold.

salmon burgers

Using a large, sharp knife, cut away any brown bits from the salmon fillet and discard, then finely chop the salmon. Place in a bowl, stir in the mustard and season to taste. Divide into 4 even-sized portions then, using slightly wet hands, shape into patties. Season the flour and use to dust the patties, shaking off any excess.

Preheat the grill to medium high to toast the ciabatta. Heat a large non-stick frying pan. Add the oil and butter and, once it starts sizzling, add the salmon burgers. Cook for 2-3 minutes on each side over a medium heat until lightly golden but a touch pink in the centre.

Toast the ciabatta rolls under the heated grill. Place the bottoms of the rolls on plates. Place the burger on top and smear the tops of the rolls with your favourite sauce.

500 g salmon, skinned and boned

2 tbsp dijon mustard

2 tbsp plain flour

4 ciabatta rolls, split in half

1 tbsp olive oil

knob unsalted butter

1 small lettuce, separated into leaves

1 small red onion, separated into rings

5

apple & honey muffins

Preheat oven to 190° C. Lightly grease one 12-cup muffin tin or line with paper muffin cups. Lightly beat egg whites.

In a separate bowl, mix dry ingredients thoroughly. In another bowl, mix together milk, oil, honey and apples. Gently fold in egg whites to the wet mixture. Add the wet mixture to the dry ingredients. Fold together until just moistened. Batter will be lumpy.

Fill greased muffin tins two-thirds full. Bake about 20 minutes until lightly browned.

2 egg whites
235 g wholemeal flour
1 tbsp baking powder
1/2 tsp salt
1 tsp ground cinnamon
170 ml skimmed milk
4 tbsp vegetable oil
4 tbsp honey
110 g chopped apples

blueberry crème brûlée

Night-before exams dessert!

Place the blueberries, apple juice and honey into the saucepan and cook gently for 10 minutes until the fruit is softened. Remove the pan from the heat and allow to cool.

Spoon cooled fruit into oven-proof ramekins or dessert bowls. Fold together the yoghurt and crème fraiche and spread over the blueberries. Chill (the mixture…) for 3 hours.

Preheat oven to high and sprinkle the sugar over the dessert mixture. Leave in oven till sugar caramelises (there should be a golden crispy coating on the top layer.)

Chill for 10 minutes in the fridge. Devour before your exam! Good luck!

340 g blueberries
1 tbsp unsweetened apple juice
1 tbsp honey
180 g plain yoghurt
180 g crème fraiche (or sour cream)
50 g sugar

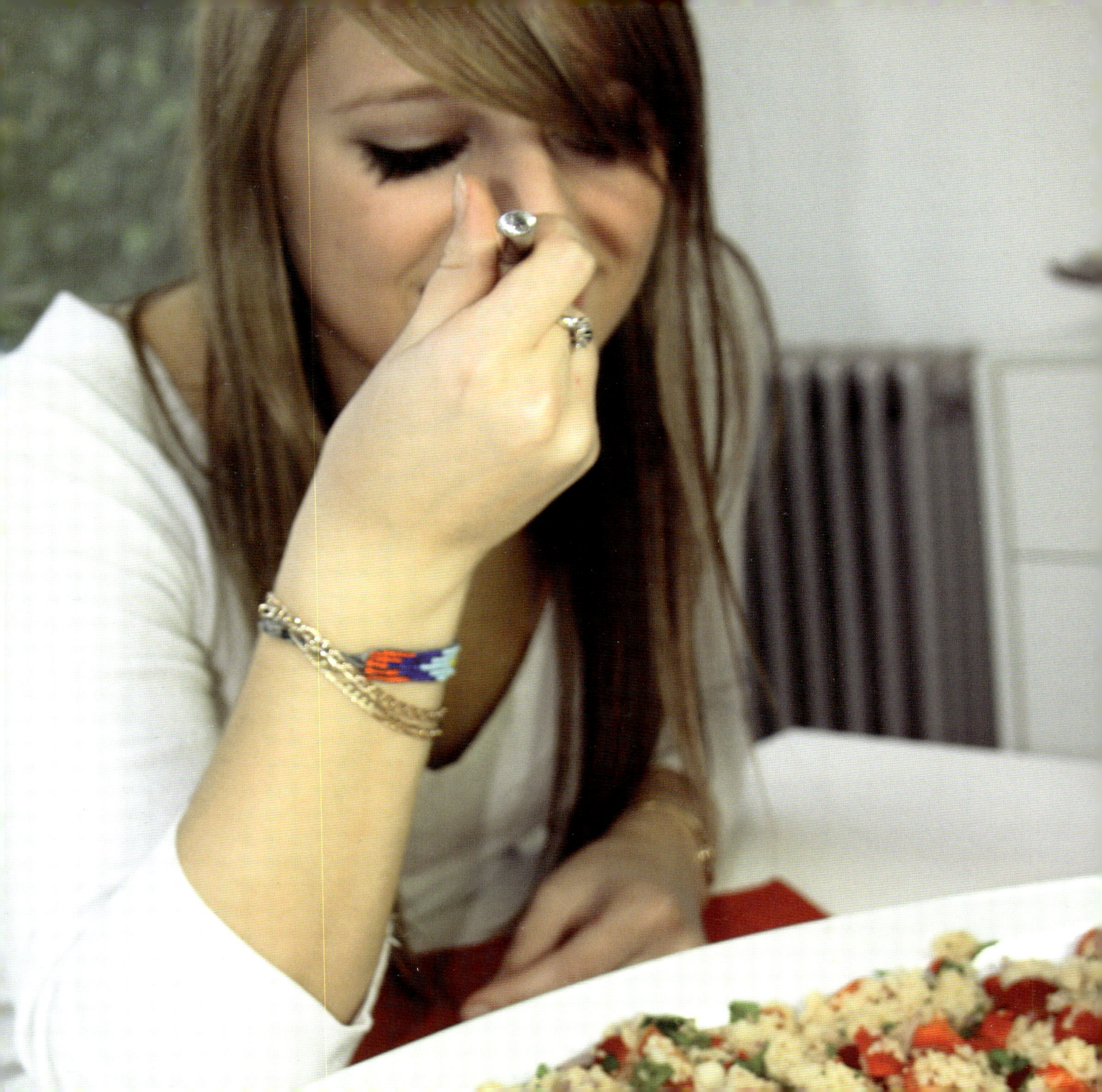

global bites

cuban black bean soup

tacos

quesadillas

fresh salsa

chili con carne

paella

spaghetti carbonara

gnocchi with gorgonzola

lemonade chicken schnizel

keftedes

tzatziki

greek salad

cous cous salad

tabouleh

greek zucchini & herb pie

hummous

kneidlach

galette des rois

bûche de nöel

1

cuban black bean soup

beans:

dried black/turtle beans (soaked overnight)
4 tbsp olive oil
4-6 cloves garlic, chopped
red onion, cut in large chunks
2 carrots, cut in large coins
1 green & 1 red pepper, diced
2 bay leaves
16 whole peppercorns
1/2 - 1 tbsp dried chilis
1 tbsp pickling spice
smoked ham hock (optional)

rice:

1 1/2 tea mugs of basmati rice
3 tea mugs of cold water
1 1/2 tsp maldon salt
6 whole cloves
6 whole peppercorns
3 crushed green cardamoms
1/3 stick whole cinnamon

condiments:

pico de gallo (mixture of chopped red onion, spring onion, red pepper, cucumber, tomato, fresh coriander, lime juice & maldon salt)
chopped haas avacado
crème fraiche
hot sauce (tabasco, etc)
guacamole (see page 71)

Black beans: Drain soaked black beans and rinse well. Sauté onion, red and green peppers and garlic in olive oil in a large saucepan until transparent. Then add beans and remainder of 'beans' ingredients and cover with cold water in a large saucepan. Cook over medium heat for 45 minutes - 1 hour, or until the beans are tender. Skim off the grey 'scum' on the surface and discard. Cook beans for 30 more minutes.

Rice: Put rice and water in a saucepan with salt and spices. Bring to a gentle boil. Partially cover with a lid until the water is gone. Remove from heat. Gently fluff the rice with a fork. Cover for 10 minutes. Serve with black beans and condiments.

Pico de gallo: Cut the red onion, spring onion, red pepper, cucumber and tomato into small dice. Add chopped coriander, the juice of one lime and a pinch of maldon salt. Mix together.

To serve: Spoon cooked rice into serving bowls, then spoon over black bean soup and add the condiments to taste. This is delicious served with fried plantain.

tacos

Grate the cheese and make the guacamole and fresh salsa in advance.

Put the olive oil, garlic and chopped onion in a large skillet over the hob. Add the minced steak and cook, stirring occasionally until well browned.   Then add the mild chili powder, tomato paste, oregano, cumin and water. Stir together and simmer for about 15 minutes.

Heat the taco shells. To serve, spoon some of the meat into the base of the shell. Add salsa, guacamole, crème fraiche, grated cheese, lettuce and tomato. Add a dash or two of hot sauce if you like things spicy.

500 g lean steak mince

3 cloves minced garlic

1 red onion, fnely chopped

1 tbsp mild chili powder

1/2 tsp maldon salt

1 tsp oregano

1/2 tsp cumin

200 g grated mature cheddar or red leceister cheese

200 g crème fraiche

fresh salsa with fresh coriander (see page 52)

guacamole (see page 71)

hot sauce (ie. tobasco, etc)

shredded iceburg lettuce

3

quesadillas

250 g tin black beans, drained
1 grilled chicken breast, sliced
1 dozen mushrooms, sliced & grilled
110 g low fat cheddar or monterrey jack cheese, shredded
8 flour tortillas
guacamole and/or sour cream

Spoon some chicken, beans and mushrooms onto the flour tortilla. Cover with cheese and top with second tortilla. Heat a frying pan to medium heat and add a small amount of oil or butter. Cook one side of quesadilla for about 1-2 minutes. Then carefully turn over and cook for another 1-2 minutes, enough time for the cheese to melt. Remove from the pan. Open quesadilla and add a spoonful of guacamole and sour cream.

4

fresh salsa

olive oil
3 cloves garlic, chopped
2 tins chopped tomatoes
2 tbsp mild chili powder
1 tsp ground cumin
3 tbsp chopped fresh coriander

Sauté three cloves of fresh garlic in 3 tbsp olive oil until transparent. Add two tins of chopped tomatoes. Bring to a simmer and add 2 tbsp mild chili powder, 2 tsp ground cumin and a large pinch of maldon salt. Simmer together for 5 minutes and cool down. When cool and ready to serve, add 3 or more tbsp chopped fresh coriander. You can add some chopped fresh chilis or tobasco or other hot sauce if you like your salsa hotter.

chilli con carne

Pour oil into the pan over medium heat, add the meat and onions, stirring every now and then, until the onions are soft and transparent and the meat has cooked. Add the minced garlic, chilli powder and cumin and cook a bit longer until the garlic is transparent. Then add the drained kidney beans and chopped tomatoes and once this just begins to boil, turn down to a slow simmer. Cook for 20 minutes and then add the polenta. Cook for another 10 minutes and the chilli is ready.

This dish is excellent re-heated and freezes very well.

750 g lean steak mince

2-3 tbsp olive or sunflower oil

4 cloves garlic, chopped

2 medium or 1 large onion, chopped

2 x 400 g tins chopped tomatoes

2 x 400 g tins kidney beans

3 tbsp mild chilli powder (this is a mixture of ground chilli, cumin & oregano from the grocery store)

1 tbsp ground cumin

3 tbsp tomato puree

75 ml water

pepper & maldon salt (to taste)

1 1/2 tbsp polenta

optional: hot sauce (i.e., tobasco)

6 paella

6 boneless chicken breasts or thighs
sea salt
freshly ground black pepper
plain flour, for dusting
olive oil
100 g chorizo, sliced
6 slices streaky bacon
1 onion, finely chopped
4 cloves of garlic, finely chopped
2 l hot chicken stock
2 large pinches of saffron
1 heaped tsp smoked paprika
500 g paella rice
small bunch flat leaf parsley, leaves picked & chopped, stalks chopped
1 1/2 handfuls peas, fresh or frozen
10 king prawns

Preheat the oven to 190° C. Season the chicken pieces with salt and pepper, and dust with flour. Heat a little olive oil in a large deep pan and fry the chicken until golden brown on both sides. Place the pieces on a baking tray and cook in the oven for 30 minutes.

Return the pan to the hob. Add the sliced chorizo and bacon and fry until browned and crispy. Then add the onion and garlic and cook until soft. Meanwhile infuse half the hot chicken stock with the saffron. Add the smoked paprika, rice and infused stock and leave to cook on a medium heat, stirring from time to time.

After 20 minutes the rice should be nearly cooked. At this point, pour in the rest of the stock along with the peas and prawns. Place a lid on the pan and cook for 10 minutes more.

Finally, add the cooked chicken and serve sprinkled with chopped parsley.

spaghetti carbonara

Cook the spaghetti in a pan of boiling salted water according to packet instructions. Once tender, drain.

While the spaghetti is cooking, fry the bacon in a frying pan until crisp.

While the bacon is frying, tip the egg yolk into a cold bowl. Add a splash of olive oil, the marjoram and sea salt and freshly ground pepper, to taste.

When the bacon is crisp, add the sliced garlic to the pan and stir well. Remove from the heat and add the drained spaghetti and egg mixture. Mix together very quickly so that the egg doesn't scramble.

Serve sprinkled with grated parmesan.

bunch of dried spaghetti, about the diameter of a 20p coin

5 slices dry-cured smoked streaky bacon, roughly chopped

1 egg yolk

generous splash of olive oil

1 tsp marjoram, chopped

sea salt

freshly ground black pepper

1/2 clove garlic, thinly sliced

freshly grated parmesan, to taste

8

gnocchi with gorgonzola

1 kg floury potatoes, such as king edwards or maris piper, unpeeled

330 g flour

1 egg, lightly beaten

250 g gorgonzola cheese

30 g butter

3 tbsp double cream

black pepper & sea salt

chopped chives, to garnish

Preheat the oven to 180° C. Put the unpeeled potatoes in a large saucepan, cover with salted water and bring to the boil. Simmer for 15-20 minutes until tender, then drain. Peel and cut in quarters. Place on a baking sheet and put it in the oven to dry for about 5 minutes.

Pass the potatoes through a coarse sieve set over a large bowl. Quickly stir in the flour and egg, and season with salt. When nicely blended, cover with a clean tea towel to retain the warmth.

Take a little of the potato mixture and roll into a long thin sausage. Slice into pieces about 2.5cm long. Using a gnocchi paddle or a fork, roll the gnocchi with your thumb. Roll it the other way to make ridges on the side.

Continue until you have used up all the potato mixture. Place the prepared gnocchi on well-floured trays as you work.

Meanwhile, bring a large pan of salted water to the boil. Drop in the gnocchi in batches. Simmer briskly for about 5 minutes until they rise to the surface. Drain gently using a wire scoop, and transfer to a warm serving dish.

While the gnocchi are cooking, melt the gorgonzola and butter in a saucepan over medium-low heat. When completely melted add the cream and boil for 1 minute.

Add the cheese mixture to the gnocchi and gently stir to mix. Sprinkle with black pepper and chopped chives and serve immediately.

lemonade chicken schnitzel

9

Mix all the marinade ingredients together and pour over the chicken fillets. Leave for a few hours, the longer the better (overnight is best).

Dip the chicken fillets into beaten egg and then into the matzo meal and salt.

Fry in a pan of hot olive oil until golden brown.

10 chicken fillets
3 large eggs beaten in matzo meal
olivie oil for frying
salt

the marinade
15 g of fresh chopped chives
12 tbsp white wine
8 tbsp of lemonade
4 crushed garlic cloves
2 tbsp of lemon juice

10   keftedes

1/2 (500 g) loaf of bread, sliced
500 g minced pork
500 g beef mince
1 egg
2 medium shallots, finely chopped
4 cloves garlic, finely chopped
1 1/2 tbsp chopped fresh mint
1 1/2 tbsp chopped fresh parsley
1 tbsp dried oregano
1/2 tbsp sea salt,
100 g plain flour, for dredging

Place the bread in a large bowl and cover with water. Set aside for about 10 minutes while you chop the shallots and herbs.

Drain the water from the bowl with the bread. Take handfuls of the bread and squeeze out as much water as possible over the sink. Place wet bread back in the bowl and add the pork, beef, egg, shallots, garlic, mint, parsley, oregano, salt and pepper. With your hands, mix all of the ingredients together thoroughly until well combined. Place in the fridge, covered, for 30 minutes to an hour (this isn't absolutely necessary, but it allows the flavours to mingle and also makes the meatballs easier to form. You could also let it sit in the fridge overnight).

Preheat the oven to 200° C. Prepare baking trays by covering with baking parchment.

Place the flour in a shallow bowl or plastic bag (however you prefer to dredge the meatballs). Take the meatball mixture from the fridge and form the meatballs: roll the mixture into 2 to 3cm balls, flatten into a disk shape, then dredge lightly in flour, shaking off any excess. Place the meatballs on the baking tray.

Bake in the preheated oven for approximately 30-40 minutes, turning over once halfway through. The meatballs should be cooked on the inside and crispy on the outside.

Serve immediately or at room temperature.

tzatziki

11

Line sieve with double thickness of cheesecloth; set over bowl.

Add yogurt. Refrigerate to drain for at least 3 hours or up to 24 hours or until reduced to about 245 g.

Peel and grate cucumber into another sieve; sprinkle with half of the salt. Let drain for 1 hour.

In small bowl, stir together drained yogurt and cucumber, remaining salt, oil, lemon juice, garlic, mint, parsley and pepper. Serve.

To serve: heat pitta bread, cut into strips and serve.

325 g plain yogurt
1/3 cucumber
1/2 tsp salt
2 tsp olive oil
2 tsp lemon juice
1 clove garlic, minced
1/4 tsp black pepper
1 tsp chopped fresh mint
1 tbsp chopped fresh flat-leaf parsley

pitta bread

12 greek salad

5 tomatoes
1 red onion
6 tbsp of olive oil
1 lemon
some parsley and mint leaves
200 g feta cheese
20 black olives (kalamata)

Cut up the tomatoes and feta into chunks and dice the red onion. Juice the lemon. (Don't forget to remove any pips from the juice.)

Warm the pita bread in the microwave or lightly toast it. Add all the ingredients into a salad bowl and serve with the warm pitta bread.

13 cous cous salad

225 g cous cous
2 tomatoes chopped small
1 red pepper
1 red onion chopped small
fresh parsley
olive oil
lemon juice

Pour 300ml of boiling water from the kettle over the couscous in a heatproof bowl. Stir with a fork. Cover with a tea towel and leave for 5 minutes.

Chop all other ingredients up into very small pieces and mix with a bit of olive oil and a drizzle with lemon juice.

Mix couscous and salad together for a delicious side dish or small meal.

tabbouleh

14

Wash and rinse the parlsey thoroughly. Shake and dry in a fresh tea towel, giving it a good shake. Cut off and discard the long stalks at the end of the bunch. Chop the parsley and put in a large bowl. Cut tomatoes in half along the 'equator' if you think of the stalk as being at the North Pole. Squeeze each tomato half so that the seeds and liquid come out and discard. Chop the tomato flesh and add to the parsley. Chop the spring onions and red onion finely and add to the mixture.

Squeeze the lemons and add this and the olive oil, salt and bulghar wheat to the bowl. Stir well and allow to sit for one hour, stirring from time to time to ensure the bulghar wheat swells and absorbs the juices. Salt to taste.

This salad keeps for one week if covered and refrigerated.

Tip: *Tomatoes are most flavourful if never refrigerated. Allow to ripen on a windowsill or table. Refrigeration destroys the flavour of the tomato.*

1 large bunch flat-leaf parsley (from the middle-eastern shop, not small packets from grocery)

4 medium tomatoes (flavourful ones such as 'on the vine' type)

6 tbsp bulghar wheat

juice of 3 lemons

maldon salt

15

greek zucchini & herb pie

1 kg zucchini (courgette), ends trimmed

salt to taste

2 tbsp extra virgin olive oil, plus additional for brushing the phyllo dough

1 large onion, finely chopped

2 garlic cloves, minced

1 large handful finely chopped dill

1 small handful chopped fresh mint, or a combination of mint and parsley

160 g crumbled feta

3 eggs, beaten

12 sheets phyllo dough

makes one 10" pie serving 8-10

Grate the zucchini using a food processor or a hand grater. Place in a large colander, salt generously and let drain for 1 hour, pressing down on it occasionally to squeeze out liquid. After an hour, squeeze out moisture (by the handful or wrap in a kitchen towel and twist the towel). Place in a bowl.

Heat 1 tbsp of the oil over medium heat in a large, heavy nonstick skillet and add the onion. Cook, stirring, until tender, about five minutes, then add the garlic. Cook, stirring, until the garlic is fragrant, about one minute. Transfer to the bowl with the zucchini. Stir in the herbs, feta, eggs and pepper. Preheat the oven to 180° C. Oil a 10" pie or cake pan.

If using filo, line the pie dish with 7 sheets, lightly brushing each sheet with oil and turning the dish after each addition so that the edges of the filo drape evenly over the pan. Fill with the zucchini mixture. Fold the draped edges in over the filling, lightly brushing the folded in sheets of filo, then layer the remaining five sheets on top, brushing each with olive oil. Stuff the edges into the sides of the pan.

Make a few slashes in the top crust so that steam can escape as the pie bakes and brush with olive oil. Bake 50-60 minutes, until the pastry is golden brown. Remove from the heat and allow to cool 15-30 minutes or to room temperature. Slice in wedges and serve. Can be reheated.

variation: *Instead of filo pastry, you can use whole wheat yeasted olive oil pie pastry, placing one rolled half into the base with the edges hanging over. Then add the mixture and place the second half on top, pressing the edges of top and bottom together to seal and form an attractive edge.*

hummous

16

Put all ingredients in a food processor and mix until well blended. Add more salt, lemon juice, tahini, garlic or cumin to taste. (optional: sprinkle with paprika and chopped parsley)

Serve with warmed pitta bread cut into strips.

1 tin of chickpeas with juice
juice of two lemons
2 cloves garlic
1 tsp maldon salt
6 tbsp light tahini
3 tbsp olive oil
1 tsp ground cumin

kneidlach

17

Put the matza meal, eggs and margerine in a large bowl and mix until smooth. Add the boiling water slowly while stirring - add more if necessary. Add two pinches of salt and one of pepper and stir again.

Wet your fingertips in the cold water and take a walnut sized amount of mixture and roll until ball shaped repeat until mixture is finished.

Boil kneidlach for 7 minutes in salted, boiling water.

Kneidlach goes well in chicken soup.

5 tbsp margerine
175g of matza meal
120 ml boiled water
240 ml room temperature water
salt & pepper
2 large eggs

18

galette des rois

125 g caster sugar
125 g ground almonds
125 g unsalted butter, softened
3 eggs
500 g puff pastry (ideally made with butter)

for the egg wash:
1 egg yolk
1 tbsp milk

Mix together the sugar and ground almonds in a bowl. Add the butter and cream it together until thoroughly mixed. Beat in the eggs one by one, mixing thoroughly between each addition.

Divide the puff pastry into two even portions. Roll out each portion and cut out two puff pastry circles, each 25cm across and 3-4mm thick. Place one puff pastry disc on a baking sheet lined with baking parchment. Make the egg wash by beating together the yolk and milk.

Spoon the almond cream into the centre of the pastry disc, leaving a 5cm edge around the diameter. Brush the edges of the pastry disc with the egg wash. Place the other pastry disc over the almond filling and seal the edges together firmly. Chill the galette des rois for 1 hour in the refrigerator. Preheat the oven to 180° C.

Brush the galette des rois with the egg wash. Using a small, sharp knife cut the edges into a scallop pattern. Using the tip of the knife cut a sun ray pattern on the top.

Bake the galette des rois for 40 minutes, until golden. Remove from the oven and brush straight away with sugar syrup.

If eating the cake to celebrate Epiphany add a small charm to the batter. Whomever ends up with the slice containing the piece is the king/queen for the day! Everyone else can clear up!

bûche de nöel

Preheat oven to 220° C. Grease and line a tin with a little vegetable oil and non-stick greaseproof paper. Cut a second piece of greaseproof paper slightly larger than the tin and sprinkle with 2 tsp sugar. Set aside.

Using a hand-held electric mixer or a wire whisk, whisk the sugar and eggs in a large bowl until very pale and light.

Sift the flour and cocoa powder together. Fold into the egg mixture gently. Pour into the prepared tin, level the surface and bake for 7-9 minutes until firm yet springy to the touch. Turn out the cake onto the sugared paper. Peel away the lining paper and trim the edges. Cover with a damp tea towel and leave to cool completely.

For the filling, whip the cream until thick and stir in the chestnut purée. Spread the cream mixture over the sponge and roll up from one long edge.

To make the chocolate butter cream, heat the sugar and water gently until the sugar dissolves, then boil rapidly until syrupy. Whisk the egg yolks, adding the sugar syrup in a steady stream, until the mixture becomes thick and pale. Add the butter and the cooled, melted chocolate. Beat in the icing sugar.

Cover the log with the butter cream and use a knife or fork to make a bark pattern. Lightly dust over the top with caster sugar.

ingredients:
few drops of vegetable oil
125 g caster sugar
4 eggs
60 g plain flour
30 g cocoa powder

filling:
90 ml double (thick) cream
45 g sweetened chestnut purée

chocolate butter cream:
90 g caster sugar
4 tbsp water
2 egg yolks
125 g softened unsalted butter
125 g sifted icing sugar
60 g plain chocolate (melted)

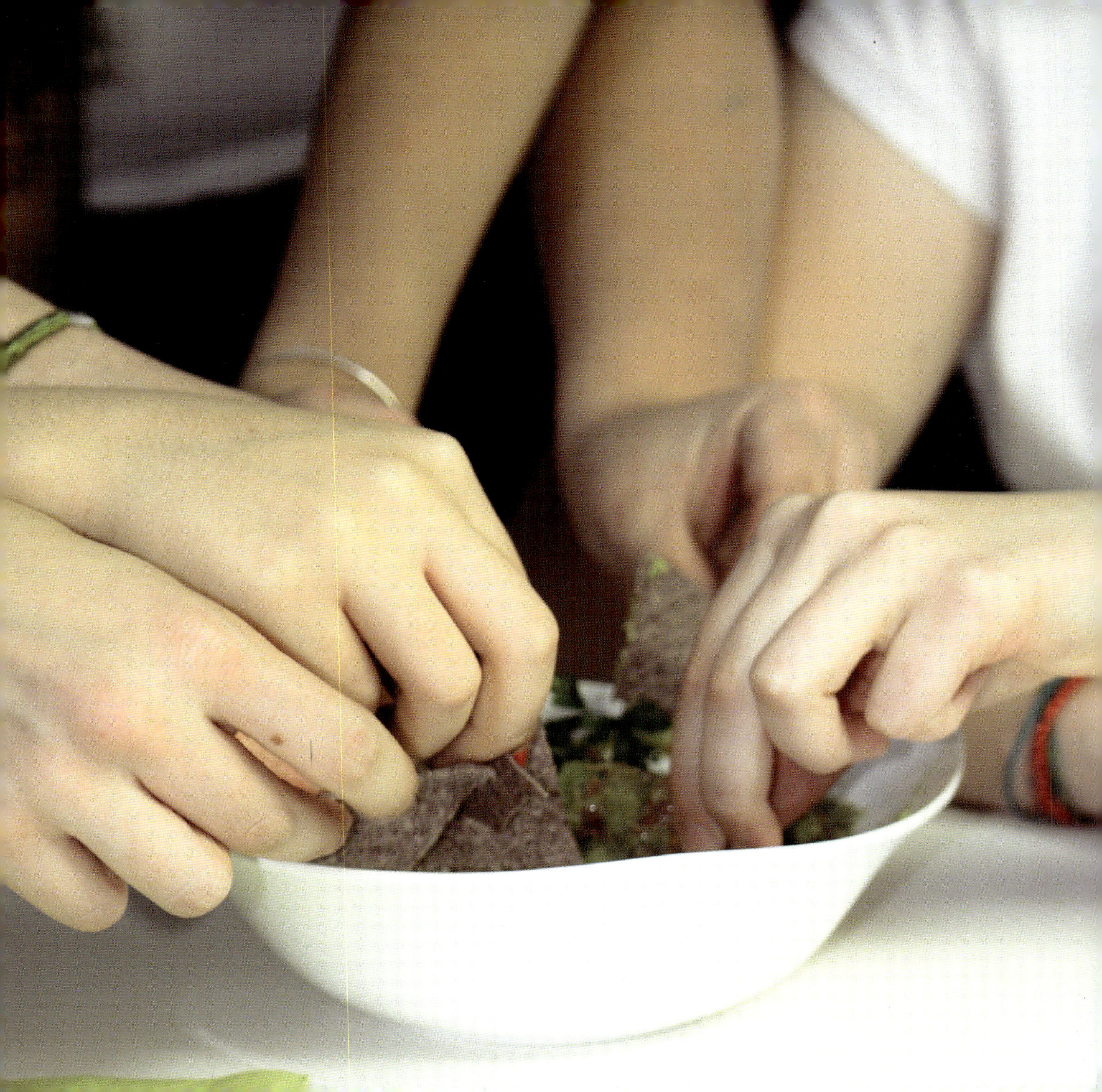

party bites

cheddar cheese straws

baked tortilla chips

cheese dreams

sandwich cut-outs

traditional pizza

easy peasy pizza

guacamole

spinach & feta parcels

sesame chicken bites

haloumi skewers

crispy veg fries

yummiest cookies ever

little christmas biscuits

rice crispy crunch

PARTY BITES

1

cheddar cheese straws

Unroll the pastry onto a floured surface and brush it with the egg mixture. Grate the cheddar over the top and push it into the pastry so that it sticks. Fold the pastry in half lengthways and brush again with egg mixture. Cut the pastry in half widthways. Put it in the fridge for 15 minutes.

Preheat the oven to 180° C. Cut the pastry into strips, then twist them for effect. Put the twists on the baking sheet and put in fridge for another 15 minutes.

Put them in the oven and bake for around 15 minutes until they are golden.

Leave to cool before eating.

1 egg yolk with 2 tbsp milk
375 g ready rolled puff pastry
50 g mature cheddar cheese
a large oiled baking sheet

2

baked tortilla chips

300 g packet old el paso corn tortillas
1 tbsp oil
3 tbsp lime juice
1 tsp chilli powder
1 tsp salt

Preheat oven to 180° C. Cut each tortilla into 8 triangular wedges and arrange in a single layer on a baking tray. In a mister or spray bottle, combine the oil and lime juice well and spray each tortilla wedge until slightly moist. (Lightly brush on the mixture if you don't have a mister.)

Combine the chilli powder and salt in a small bowl and sprinkle on the wedges. Bake for about 7 minutes. Rotate the tray and bake for another 8 minutes or until the wedges are crisp, but not too brown. Serve warm or room temperature with salsas, dips or guacamole.

cheese dreams

3

Toast or grill slices of bread on one side only.

Spread untoasted side with a dash of tomato puree and a little mustard (if desired). Cover with grated cheese.

Place under hot grill and watch – take care, they will brown very quickly.

Cut into fingers.

2 slices white or brown bread from sliced loaf
75 g hard cheese eg cheddar, grated
tomato puree
mustard *(optional)*

serves 2

sandwich cut-outs

4

Make your favourite sandwiches using whole grain bread, and cut into fun party/festive shapes with cookie cutters.

slices of white or brown bread
fillings of your choice
cookie cutters

5

traditional pizza

pizza dough (recipe makes enough dough for two 10 inch pizzas):

240 ml warm water

1 package (2tsp) of active dry yeast

260 g bread flour (normal flour is also fine)

2 tbsp olive oil

2 tsp salt

1 tsp sugar

pizza ingredients:

olive oil

tomato sauce

mozarella or parmesan cheese shredded

mushrooms

green peppers

italian sausage (precooked)

basil

pesto

onions

pepperoni

sliced ham

Method for dough making: Pour warm water in a large mixing bowl. Sprinkle on yeast and let sit for 5 minutes until dissolved. Stir to speed up the dissolving process. Attach a mixing paddle to the mixer and mix in the olive oil, flour, salt and sugar on a low speed setting for a minute. Remove the mixing paddle and replace with a dough hook. Knead using the mixer and dough hook on a medium speed until the dough is smooth and elastic (approx. 10 mins). *Tip: If you don't have a mixer you can mix and knead by hand!* Place the ball of dough in a bowl that has been coated lightly with olive oil. Turn the dough around so it's covered in oil. Cover with cling film. Leave in a warm place (23-30° C) until the dough has doubled in size (1-1 1/2 hours).

Method for pizza making: Remove the cling film from the dough and punch the dough until it deflates. Divide the dough in half and form two round balls of dough. Place each in a bowl and cover and leave for 10 minutes. Prepare the toppings (tip: don't go overboard!). Take one ball of dough and flatten with your hands on a lightly floured work space. Starting at the centre and working outwards, use your fingertips to press the dough to 1/2 inch thick. Turn and stretch the dough until it will not stretch further. Let the dough relax for 5 mins and then continue to stretch till it reaches the diameter you want (10" is recommended). You can pinch the edges to form an edge. Brush the top of the dough with olive oil. Use your fingers to press down and make dents along the surface of the dough to prevent bubbling and let rest for 5 minutes. Repeat for second ball of dough. Put toppings onto pizza. Bake the pizzas until the crust is browned and the cheese is golden (this should take 10-15 minutes!) Remove pizzas from oven.

PARTY BITES

easy peasy pizza

6

Preheat the oven to 200° C (gas mark 6). Using the naan bread as your pizza base, place on a baking tray.
Slice the tomatoes, and place on top of the naan bread along with the mozzarella and red Leicester cheeses. Then place in the oven.

After about 10 minutes, remove from the oven, and garnish with a bit of black pepper and coriander before serving.

naan bread
40 g loose tomatoes
20 g italian mozzarella
4 g red leicester cheese
black pepper
corriander

guacamole

7

Cut the avocados in half and reserve two stones. With your knife, make lots of scores in the flesh of the avacodoes, cutting nearly to the skin. Then with a large spoon, scoop out the flesh into a bowl. Add the garlic, lime juice, ground cumin and salt. Mash some with a fork, lumps are fine. Then stir in the tomatoes and adjust the mixture with seasonings until it is to your liking.

Tip: *to delay the guacamole turning dark, place a couple of the stones into the mixture, then cover with cling film.*

3 ripe haas avocados
2 cloves garlic (mashed)
juice of 3 limes
1 tsp ground cumin
1 tsp maldon salt
2 fresh (de-seeded) tomatoes, diced

8

spinach & feta parcels

For the spinach/feta filling:
4 tbsp olive oil
400 g thawed frozen spinach
1 finely chopped onion
1 tbsp oregano
4 tbsp fresh mint, chopped
salt & pepper
200 g feta cheese – crumbled
50 ml half-fat crème fraiche
270 g box filo pastry (thawed)

60 g melted butter (or olive oil)

Pour olive oil in a large frying pan over medium heat on the hob and add chopped garlic and onions and sauté until transparent. Add chopped spinach, mint and oregano and stir together for 10 minutes. Turn off heat and allow to cool slightly, then add crème fraiche, feta and pepper. Add salt to taste.

Melt butter in small saucepan. Lay out the stack of thawed filo pastry sheets and put one on a baking tray. Paint with butter (or olive oil) and repeat this process using two more sheets. Cut the pastry sheets into 6 equal rectangles.

In the centre of each rectangle, place about 1-2 tbsp of the spinach/feta mixture. Pull up two opposite corners of the filo rectangles and pinch together then the other two corners. Brush the parcels with more melted butter or olive oil just before baking.

These can be made in advance and stored in a fridge for a couple of days or in the freezer for a couple of months. To freeze, it is best to freeze on a tray and then put in a freezer bag once frozen. The parcels can be cooked without the need to defrost.

sesame chicken bites

Mix everything together in a big bowl except the sesame seeds.

Wet your hands and roll the mixture into small balls in your hands (a little smaller than a golf ball).

Roll each ball into a dish with the sesame seeds in it.

Fry the chicken bits in oil until cooked.

Tip: *for a yummy sauce, mix 2 tablespoons of sweet chilli sauce with 3 tablespoons of soy sauce, 1 tablespoon of teriyaki sauce and a pinch of sugar.*

500 g minced chicken
2 teaspoons teriyaki sauce
2 teaspoons soy sauce
1/2 teaspoon caster sugar
2 eggs
half a grated onion
260 g sesame seeds

PARTY BITES

10

haloumi skewers

Put cut cheese and veggies into a big bowl.

Pour oil, garlic, lemon and herbs. Stir to cover it and leave for about 10 minutes.

Line the grill pan with foil and preheat the grill to high.

Stick cheese and veggies onto metal or wooden skewers. (if you're using wooden skewers make sure you soak them for at least 20 minutes before hand in water so that they don't catch alight!)

Grill on the rack. Turn every few minutes for 8-10 minutes.

Drizzle more marinade if they're looking dry. Cook until the cheese is hot and soft and the veggies are soft but a little crispy.

Add the remaining marinade and serve up ready to impress!

Serves 4

450 g haloumi cheese, cubed
8 mushrooms
2 red peppers cut into pieces
4 tomatoes cut into pieces
2 red onions cut into pieces
and any other veggies you wish to add

marinade:
5 tbsps olive oil
2 cloves garlic, crushed
2 tbsps lemon
2 pinches of fresh chopped parsley or basil
8-12 skewers

11 crispy veg fries

Mix the seasoning into the flour. Make a well in the centre and gradually mix in the egg, followed by the milk and oil.

Finely dice the vegetables and drain the sweetcorn thoroughly. Stir the vegetable evenly into the batter.

Heat a little oil in a frying pan and add a tablespoonful of mixture at a time to the pan, turning to brown evenly.

Drain immediately on kitchen paper. The idea is to keep the fresh, crisp texture of the vegetables as much as possible.

115 g plain wholemeal flour
1 free range egg
150 ml milk
a little sunflower oil
1 small tin sweetcorn
1 small green pepper or any other crisp veg such as celery or courgette

12 yummiest cookies ever

Mix the butter, sugars and vanilla until light in colour and fluffy. Slowly beat in the eggs. Sift in flour and bicarbonate of soda.

Spoon out onto a tray into slightly flattened balls on greaseproof paper (or a greased surface). Cook for 12-15 minutes at 150-170° C or until the cookies are barely puffed and only coloured at the edges.

Tip: *if you have any spare dough keep it in the fridge for a while to make the cookies extra chewy. Or put in the freezer for another day.*

225 g unsalted butter - soft
375 g light soft brown sugar
50 g caster sugar
3 tsp vanilla extract
2 large eggs
400 g plain flour
2 tsp bicarbonate of soda
150 g chocolate chips

13 little christmas biscuits

225 g soft butter
2 tsp ground ginger
2 tsp ground cinnamon
1 egg
175 g brown sugar
1 tsp bicarbonate of soda
350 g plain flour
1 tsp mixed spice
icing sugar for dusting

makes 50

Preheat the oven to 190° C.

Mix together the butter and brown sugar in a food processor for a few minutes. Add the egg and mix again.

Sift in the flour, spices, bicarbonate of soda, and mix until dough is formed.

Knead the mixture gently on a floured surface, roll into a ball and cover with cling film and chill in fridge for an hour.

Divide into two parts and roll each part out onto separate sheets of baking parchment to 0.5 cm thick.

Cut into the dough or use cutters to create Christmas themed shapes until all dough is used.

Bake in the oven for 10 minutes or until golden brown around the edges.

Remove from oven and leave to cool.

Dust with icing sugar to create a Christmas effect.

rice crispy crunch

14

Break up the chocolate into small chunks and place in bowl.

Microwave until melted. If no microwave is available, fill a saucepan with 2.5 cm of water until almost boiled. Then place a heat-proof bowl into the saucepan and stir the chocolate until melted.

Add the rice crispies to the bowl and stir toll the chocolate crispies are completely mixed. *Hint: Add the crispies slowly till the mixture is thick (test thickness by placing the mixture on a spoon… if it stays then it is time to move to the next step. If not then continue adding crispies.)*

Spoon the mixture into the paper cake cups. Place the tray of cupcakes into the fridge for an hour till the chocolate has hardened. (Whilst you're waiting…lick the spoon clean and clear up.)

Open fridge and enjoy.

For a twist add marshmallows to the mixture or experiment with different cereals.

100 g bar chocolate (milk/dark/white)

90 g rice crispies

60 g unsalted butter (optional - for more flavour)

equipment: spoon, 12 paper cups
preparation time: 20 minutes

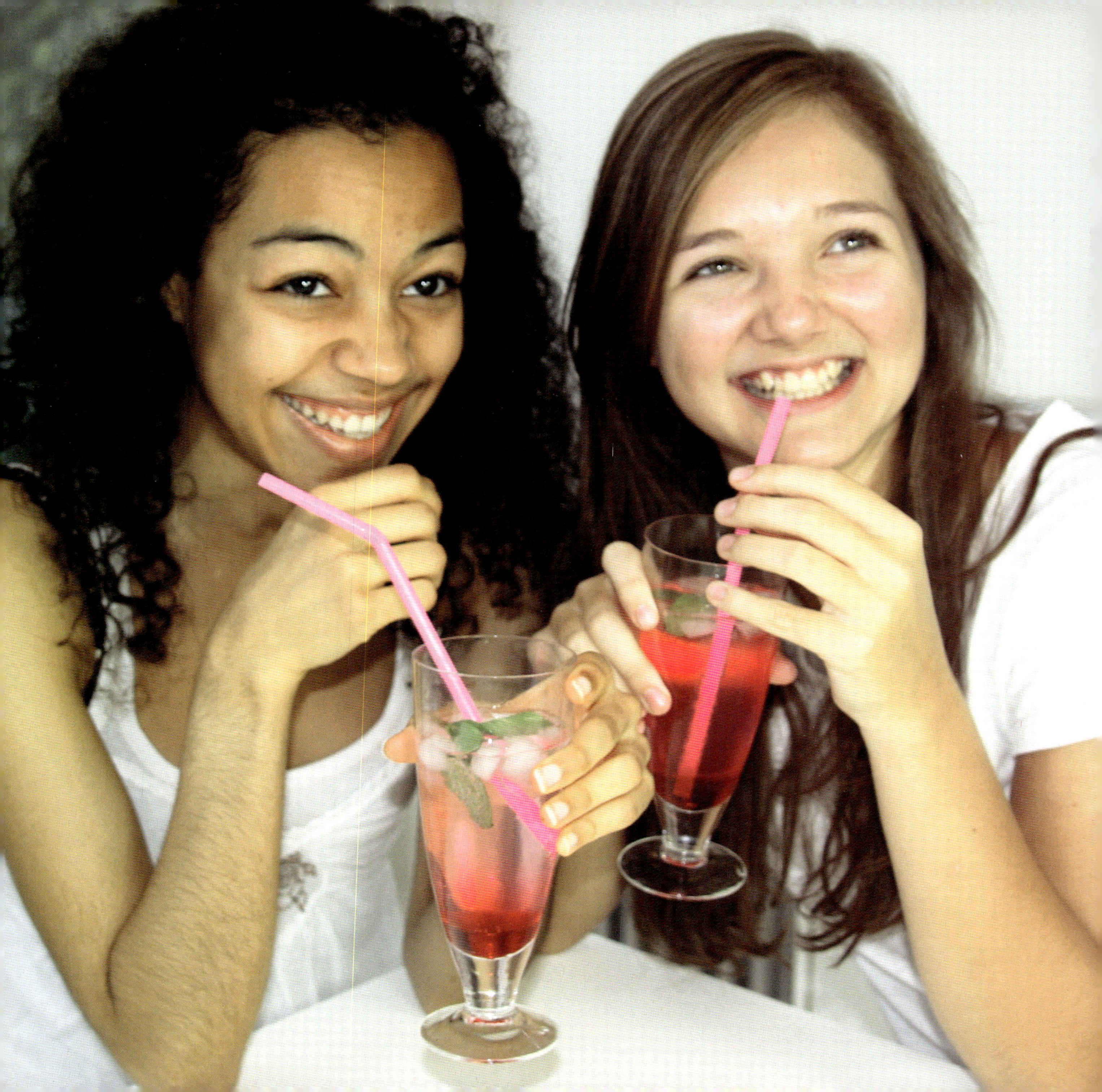

liquid bites

breakfast brain-booster

banana & honey breakfast smoothie

as you like it smoothie

tropical dream smoothie

no moo smoothie

valerian hot chocolate

indian rose & lime chiller

oreo milkshake

peanut butter & banana milkshake

pomegranate & orange sunrise

mai tai mocktail

virgin mary

piña colada mocktail

LIQUID BITES

1

breakfast brain booster

240 ml orange juice
1/2 banana, cut into pieces
10 fresh strawberries; hulled
3 ice cubes

Combine all the ingredients in your blender.
Blend until thick and frothy and pour into a tall glass for your healthy breakfast.

2

banana & honey breakfast smoothie

150 ml skimmed/semi-skimmed milk
250 ml low fat plain yoghurt
2 tbsp crushed ice
1 tbsp honey
1 banana

Place everything in a blender and whizz!

3

as you like it smoothie

1 tbsp ground seeds or nuts (almonds, pine nuts)
natural yoghurt
fresh fruit (blueberries, plums, apricots, banana etc)

Blend all the ingredients in a blender.
Pour into glass.
Enjoy!

Experiment by adding ice-cream to the mix to make a milkshake for dessert.

tropical dream smoothie

4

Combine all ingredients in a mixer except for the honey. Whirl for approximately 15 seconds. Pour in the optional protein powder and/or honey and spin for 10 seconds.

6 large chunks of juicy pineapple
6 strawberries
1/2 crushed mango
1 crushed passion fruit
1/2 crushed banana
100 ml apple juice
1/2 freshly squeezed orange
a couple of handfuls crushed ice
If you want something sweeter & creamier add a glass of milk or vanilla yogurt
1 tbsp honey (optional)
1 scoop protein powder (optional)

no moo smoothie

5

Soak the cashew nuts overnight in cold water. Drain the nuts and place in a blender along with the water. Blend together until it becomes a smooth nutty 'milk'.

Peel and de-stone the mango, chop the flesh roughly and add the chunks to the blender. Blend again.

When finished, stir in the linseed.

serves 2

60 g shelled cashew nuts
180 ml water
1 ripe mango
1 1/2 tsp linseeds

6

valerian hot chocolate

3 tbsp fresh valerian root
3 tbsp fresh lemon balm leaves
3 tsp fresh lavender leaves
1 tsp mint
6 leaves & 3 heads from passion flowers
zest of 1 1/2 oranges
900 ml whole milk
50 g dark chocolate
dash of vanilla extract

Chop off the top and bottom from the fresh valerian root. Add the valerian root, lemon balm leaves, lavender flowers, passion flowers, orange zest, mint, and milk into a heavy-based pan and gently heat for 5-10 minutes. Strain through a fine sieve.

Return the strained milk back into the pan, then stir in the dark chocolate and vanilla over a low heat for 3-4 minutes, or until melted.

Pour into mugs and drink immediately.

7

indian rose & lime chiller

1 tbsp rose syrup
200 ml tonic water or club soda
juice of 1/2 lime
fresh mint leaves
ice

Fill a tall glass with ice cubes. Pour the rose syrup into the glass and add the tonic or soda water. Do not stir.

Squeeze the lime juice into to the glass. Finally, garnish with a sprig of mint.

Tasty stuff.

LIQUID BITES

oreo milkshake
8

Combine ice-cream, cookies and milk in a blender.

Blend on medium speed for about 2 minutes or until well combined.

3 scoops of vanilla ice-cream
3-5 crushed Oreo cookies
180 ml ounces milk.

peanut butter & banana milkshake
9

Blend all the ingredients together in a blender.

250 ml milk
1 ripe banana, peeled
ice cubes
2 tbsp crunchy peanut butter
1/2 tsp pure vanilla extract

pomegranate & orange sunrise
10

Half fill two cocktail glasses with ice, divide the orange juice between them. Your glass should be about 2/3 full.

Very slowly, to make sure it sinks to the bottom, pour the pomegranate juice equally between the two glases.

Garnish with a slice of orange.

ice
400 ml freshly squeezed orange juice
160 ml pure pomegranate juice
2 thin slices of orange

LIQUID BITES

11

120 ml pineapple juice
120 ml cranberry juice
2 tsp lime juice
crushed ice

mai tai mocktail

Place crushed ice at the bottom of glass. Pour ingredients, stir, and serve. To garnish, float a thin slice of pineapple on the top of the glass.

12

300 ml tomato juice
tabasco sauce (to taste)
worcestershire sauce (to taste)
salt & pepper
lemon
celery stick

virgin mary

Half fill a cocktail shaker with ice, add 300ml of tomato juice, between 2-10 dashes of Tabasco sauce, (according to your hot pepper tolerance), 2-3 dashes of Worcestershire sauce, the juice of quarter of a lemon and a quick grind of salt and pepper. Shake and strain into an ice-filled glass. Garnish with a small stick of celery.

13

200 ml tbsp pineapple juice
60 ml tbsp coconut cream
1 glass of crushed ice

piña colada mocktail

Mix together the pineapple juice and coconut cream. Pour over crushed ice.

starbites

alfie allen

mandy wagstaff

girls aloud's kimberly walsh

lily allen

meg rosoff

nigella lawson

the saturdays' rochelle wiseman

1

2 skinless chicken breasts

1 lemon

olive oil

salt

black pepper

pasta (penne is best)

pesto (I usually buy this at a good italian deli but if you're feeling keen you can make it fresh with basil leaves, pine nuts and olive oil)

parmesan

chicken pesto pasta aka alfie allen speciality

Slice the chicken breasts into fillets lengthways and marinate for a few hours in the lemon juice and olive oil. Place the fillets on a griddle and brush with more olive oil and lemon juice. Meanwhile cook the pasta and drain when cooked. Mix in the pesto and some extra parmesan cheese to taste. Cut the fillets (they should be golden-browned) into bite size pieces and mix into the pasta.

Serve with extra parmesan and black pepper.

Yum yum there will be none left.

mandy wagstaff's lemon drizzle cake

170 g self-raising flour
170 g caster sugar
110 g butter, softened
2 large eggs, beaten
75 ml milk
1 tsp lemon zest

1 lemon
80 g caster sugar

Butter the base and sides of a 7-8 inch cake tin and line the base with a disc of greaseproof paper.

Pre-heat the oven to 170° C.

Place the flour, sugar and butter in a large mixing bowl. Add the eggs, milk and lemon zest. Mix with an electric whisk or wooden spoon until everything is combined and the butter is smooth. Spoon into the prepared tin and bake in the pre-heated oven for 45-50 minutes until the cake is well risen and golden.

Leave to cool for 10 minutes. Remove from the tin and score the top lightly with a knife.

Meanwhile mix the lemon juice with the remaining sugar and spoon over the cake allowing it to seep in.

Enjoy!

copyright © 2010 Mandy Wagstaff

3

115 g butter or margarine

170 g sugar (granulated, caster or mix in some demerara)

225 g self raising flour

2 eggs

2 large or 3 medium very ripe bananas

girls aloud kimberly walsh's banana cake recipe

Heat the oven to 180° C.
Grease a 2 lb loaf tin.
Mash the bananas with a sturdy fork.
Cream the butter and sugar together and mix in the eggs.
Mix together the banana mush and the other mixture.
Mix in the flour.
Scrape into the loaf tin and bake for 40 minutes.
Lower the temperature to 150° C and cook for a further 30 minutes.
Let it cool turned out on a rack before devouring it.

Tip: ideal for using up bananas that you've kept for a bit too long!

lily allen's granny mary's cheese pie

4

2 tins of spaghetti in tomato sauce
potatoes for mashing
mature cheddar cheese, grated
loads of butter & pepper

This recipe is a one of those crazy family recipes handed down, every family has one. It sounds really gross but is actually totally yummy. It was created by my Granny Mary Owen and my mum also made it all the time and I still like it as comfort food to eat on the sofa watching tv.

Put the spaghetti in a dish. Peel and cook potatoes until soft then mash or puree with masses of butter and pepper. Add the grated cheese, saving some to sprinkle on the top. Level out and make swirls with fork, sprinkle cheese, grate more pepper. You can also add some slices of tomato, mum sometimes does but actually I always pick them off. Then put in oven with the grill setting on so it browns a bit on top.

Yum yum yum.

5

150 g sugar
115 g unsalted butter
125 g unbleached flour, sifted
1 tsp baking powder
pinch of salt
2 eggs
24 halves pitted purple plums
sugar & cinnamon for topping

meg rosoff's plum torte

from the New York Times in about 1982 -- still incredibly delicious

Total time: 1 hour 15 minutes

Preheat oven to 180º C degrees.
Cream sugar and butter in a bowl. Add flour, baking powder, salt and eggs, and beat well.
Spoon the batter into a spring form of 8, 9 or 10 inches.
Place the plum halves skin side up on top of the batter.
Sprinkle lightly with sugar, depending on the sweetness of the fruit.
Bake for 40 to 50 minutes. Cool to lukewarm, and serve with ice-cream or cream.

Serves 8

nigella lawson's goujons of sole

I prefer to fry only a few at a time using a small saucepan, such as one you'd boil a breakfast egg in, rather than having to heat a huge, frightening vat-ful of oil.

Cut the sole fillets in half lengthways, and then slice each fillet half into about four long strips on the diagonal. This will give you eight goujons from each fillet.

Put the cornflour into a shallow bowl and season with salt and pepper. Put the breadcrumbs or panko into another shallow bowl, and beat the eggs in an additional bowl.

Dip each goujon into the seasoned cornflour, coating it well, then the beaten egg, and finally the breadcrumbs.

Lay the goujons on a cooling rack for a while, and heat the oil in a pan. I use a small one (approx milkpan size) (Or at this point you can freeze them in layers of baking parchment in an airtight container).

Fry the goujons, in batches of about 3, for about 2 minutes, or until crisp and golden. Remove to pieces of kitchen paper as you go, to get rid of excess oil.

Adapted from Nigella Express *published by Chatto & Windus*

6

OK, so these may be just fancy fish fingers, but then again, "just" is probably not the right word. They are gorgeous and tender within, and fry to a gratifying crunch on the golden-crumbed exterior. I actually boost the quantities below, preparing more than one meal-ful at a time. Breading the many strips of fish can get a bit monotonous (although there is a lot to be said for boring, repetitive activity to decompress a busy brain) but the advantage is you can stash them in the freezer and then cook from frozen, which means you've got a near instant, delicious, brain-boosting meal for any teatime during the school week - or whenever you feel the urge.

2 lemon sole fillets, skinned

70 g cornflour

100 g breadcrumbs or panko (Japanese breadcrumbs that comes in packets)

2 eggs

250 ml groundnut or grapeseed oil, or as needed (depending on size of pan)

salt & pepper

Makes 16, enough for about 3 people as a main course, depending on age and appetite of eater!

7

the saturdays rochelle wiseman's favourite pasta

vegetable oil
2 large onions
3 garlic cloves
1 kg minced beef
2 tins chopped tomatoes
button mushrooms
1 tsp dried oregano
1 tsp dried thyme
dried spaghetti
parmesan

Fry the onions and garlic and the oil

Add the beef and fry until cooked

Add the mushrooms until they are soft

Add the tomatoes and herbs

Boil the pasta for 10 minutes

Serve and add cheese on top

sponsors of the book

demista™

fairacre properties

philip ross solicitors

cyplon holidays

savills

remedica

eurobank efg

yva solicitors

specific films

carlton books

goldstone perl research

A huge thank you from the **bite me** team for your outstanding support. We could not have done it without you.

friends of the book

giselle & michael green

freddie green

phoebe green

sara burns

the perl family

george christofides

carolos georgallis

kallis & co.

hyde park agencies

cypressa

titan insurance agencies ltd

nakis papadopoulos

the superheroes

arabella & lucinda neagle

helena nathan-king

alg accountants

the o'connor family

printed by europaprint london